Clairvoyance and Psychic Abilities

By
C. W. Leadbeater
Annie Besant

Copyright © 2020 Lamp of Trismegistus. All rights reserved. No part of this publication may be reproduced or transmitted in any form or by any means, electronic or mechanical, including photocopying, recording, or by any information storage and retrieval system, without permission in writing from Lamp of Trismegistus. Reviewers may quote brief passages.

ISBN: 978-1-63118-403-1

Esoteric Classics

Other Books in this Series and Related Titles

The Hymns of Hermes by G. R. S. Mead (978-1-63118-405-5)

Yoga, Hatha-Yoga and Raja-Yoga by Annie Besant (978-1-63118-476-5)

Tao Te Ching & Commentary by Lao Tzu & C Johnston (978-1-63118-495-6)

Buddhist Psalms by Shinran (978-1-63118-465-9)

Gnosis of the Mind by G. R. S. Mead (978-1-63118-408-6)

The Machinery of the Mind by Dion Fortune (978-1-63118-451-2)

Catholicism, Yoga and Hinduism by Hartmann &c (978-1-63118-478-9)

The Crest-Jewel of Wisdom by Adi Shankara (978-1-63118-475-8)

A Collection of Early Writings on Astral Travel (978-1-63118-477-2)

The Path of Light: A Manual of Maha-Yana Buddhism (978-1-63118-471-0)

The Golden Verses of Pythagoras: Five Translations (978-1-63118-479-6)

The Human Aura: Astral Colors and Thought Forms (978-1-63118-419-2)

The Book of the Watchers by Enoch (978-1-63118-416-1)

The Hymn of Jesus by G. R. S. Mead (978-1-63118-492-5)

The Poem of Hashish by A Crowley & C Baudelaire (978-1-63118-484-0)

Qabbalistic Teachings and the Tree of Life by M P Hall (978-1-63118-482-6)

Rosicrucian Rules, Secret Signs, Codes and Symbols by various (978-1-63118-488-8)

The Star and the Garter by Aleister Crowley (978-1-63118-406-2)

The Sepher Yetzirah and the Qabalah by M P Hall (978-1-63118-481-9)

History and Teachings of the Rosicrucians by W W Westcott &c (978-1-63118-487-1)

The Leadbeater Reader: A Selection of Occult Essays (978-1-63118-483-3)

Audio versions are also available on Audible, Amazon and Apple

Table of Contents

Introduction...7

How Clairvoyance is Developed
By C. W. Leadbeater...9

Psychic and Spiritual Development
By Annie Besant...33

Psychic Powers
By C. W. Leadbeater...47

Psychism and Spirituality
By Annie Besant...57

INTRODUCTION

The word "esoteric" can be difficult to define. Esotericism in general can be seen less as a system of beliefs and more as a category, which encompasses numerous, different systems of beliefs. It's a bit of juxtaposition, since the word "esoteric" indicates something that few people know about, while the term itself broadly covers numerous philosophies, practices, areas of study and belief systems.

In a greater sense, Esotericism acts as a storehouse for secret knowledge, which is often considered ancient (*by tradition, if not by fact*), passed down from generation to generation, in private. At various times in history, simply possessing the knowledge of some of these subjects, was considered illegal and a jailable offence, if discovered. This usually included such general topics as Alchemy, Pharmacology, Qabalah, Hermeticism, Occultism, Ceremonial Magic, Astrology, Divination, Rosicrucianism and so on. Collectively, these areas of study were often referred to as the esoteric sciences.

Sometimes, the outer garment of a subject isn't esoteric, while what is hidden beneath it, is. As an example, Freemasonry isn't necessarily esoteric by nature (at *least not anymore*), but certain signs, passwords and handshakes given to the candidate during their initiation, are in fact, esoteric, in the sense that they are hidden from the general public.

Today, in the twenty-first century, such topics are readily available at bookstores across the country, and numerous mainsteam publishers offer beginners guides and coffee-table volumes on many of these subjects, intended for mass appeal. Books like *"The Secret"* have turned previously arcane topics into household knowledge. All that being the case, however, it isn't to say that there still aren't buried secrets to uncover, ancient wisdom being ignored and forgotten mysteries to be explored. In fact, it is often that we are only able to further our own studies by standing on the shoulders of these disappearing giants.

Lamp of Trismegistus is doing its part to help preserve humanity's esoteric history by making some of these classics available to those students who are seeking to unearth the knowledge of these ancient colossi.

So, be sure to check other titles from our *Esoteric Classics* series, as well as our *Occult Fiction, Theosophical Classics, Foundations of Freemasonry Series, Supernatural Fiction, Paranormal Research Series, Studies in Buddhism* and our *Christian Apocrypha Series.* You can also download the audio versions of most of these titles from Amazon, Apple or Audible, for learning on the go.

HOW CLAIRVOYANCE IS DEVELOPED

By C. W. Leadbeater

When a man has studied the subject of clairvoyance sufficiently to realize that the claims made on its behalf are true, his next enquiry usually is "How can I gain this power for myself? If this faculty be latent in every man, as you say, how can I so develop myself as to bring it into motion, and so have direct access to all this knowledge of which you tell me?" In reply we can assure him that this thing can be done, and that it has been done. There are even many ways in which the faculty may be gained, though most of them are unsafe and eminently undesirable, and there is only one that can be thoroughly and unreservedly recommended to all men alike. But that we may understand the subject, and see where lie the dangers that have to be avoided, let us consider exactly what it is that has to be done.

In the case of all cultured people belonging to the higher races of the world, the faculties of the astral body are already fully developed, as I have explained in earlier lectures. But we are not in the least in the habit of using them; they have slowly grown up within us during the ages of our evolution, but they have come to us so gradually that we have not as yet realized our powers, and they are still to a great extent untried weapons in our hands. The physical faculties, to which we are thoroughly accustomed, overshadow these others and hide their very existence, just as the nearer light of the sun hides from our eyes the light of the far-distant stars. So that there are two things to be done if we wish to enter into this part of our heritage as evolved human beings; we must keep our too-insistent physical faculties out of the way for the time, and we must habituate ourselves to the employment of these others, which are as yet unfamiliar to us.

The first step, then, is to get the physical senses out of the way for the present. There are many ways of doing this, but broadly they all range themselves under two heads - one comprising methods by which they are forced out of the way by temporary violent suppression, and the other including methods, much slower, but infinitely surer, by which we ourselves gain permanent control over them. Most of the methods of violent suppression are injurious to the physical body, to a greater or less extent, and they all have certain undesirable characteristics in common. One of these is that they leave the man in a passive condition, able perhaps to use his higher senses, but with very little choice as to how he shall employ them, and to a large extent undefended against any unpleasant or evil influence, which he may happen to encounter. Another characteristic is that any power gained by these methods can at best be only temporary. Many of them confer it only during the limited period of their action, and even the best of them can only dower the man with certain faculties during this one physical life. In the East, where they have studied these matters for so many centuries, they divide methods of development into two classes, just as I have done, and they call them by the names laukika and lokothra, the first being the "worldly" or temporary method, any results gained by which will inhere only in the personality, and therefore by available only for this present physical life, while whatever is obtained by the second process is gained by the ego, the soul, the true man, and so is a permanent possession for evermore, carried over from one earthly life to another. For most methods of the former class little training is required, and when there is training it is of the vehicles only, and so at the best it can affect only this present set of vehicles, and when the man returns into incarnation with a fresh set all his trouble will be lost; whereas by the second method it is the soul itself which is trained in the control of its vehicles, and naturally it can apply the power and the knowledge thus gained to its new vehicles in the next life. Let me mention to you first some of the undesirable ways in which clairvoyance is developed in various countries.

Among non-Aryan tribes in India it is often obtained by the use of drugs - bhang, hashish, and others of the same kind. These stupefy the physical body something as anesthetics do, and thus the man in his astral vehicle is set free as he would be in sleep, but with far less possibility of being awakened. Before taking the drug, the man has set his mind strongly on the endeavor to train his astral senses into activity, and so as soon as he is free he tries to use his faculties, and with practice he succeeds to some extent. When he awakens his physical body, he remembers more or less of his visions, and tries to interpret them, and in that way he often obtains a great reputation for clairvoyance and prevision. Sometimes while in his trance, he may be spoken through by some dead man, just as any other medium may be. There are others who obtain the same condition by inhaling stupefying fumes, usually produced by the burning of a mixture of drugs. It is probable that the clairvoyance of the pythonesses of old was often of this type. It is stated in the case of one of the most celebrated of those oracles of ancient days, the priestess sat always upon a tripod over a crack in the rock, out of which vapor ascended. After breathing this vapor for a time, she became entranced, and some one then spoke through her organs in the ordinary way so familiar to the visitors to séances. It is not difficult for us to see how undesirable both these methods are from the point of view of real development.

Probably most of us have heard of the dancing dervishes, one part of whose religion consists in this curious dance of ecstasy, in which they whirl round and round in a kind of frenzy until vertigo seizes them and they eventually fall insensible to the ground. In that trance, worked up as they are by religious fervor, they frequently have most extraordinary visions, and are able to some extent to experience and remember lower astral conditions. I have seen something of this, and also of the practices of the Obeah or Voodoo votaries among the Negroes; but these latter are usually connected with magical ceremonies, loathsome, indecent, horrible, such as none of us would dream of touching for any purpose, whatever results might be promised to us. Yet they certainly do produce results under favorable conditions, though not such results as any of us could possibly wish to obtain. Indeed, none of the methods mentioned so far would at all commend themselves to us, though I have heard of Europeans who have experimented with the Oriental drugs.

Nevertheless we also have undesirable methods in the West - methods of self-hypnotization, which should be carefully avoided by all who wish to develop in purity and safety. A person may be told to gaze for some time at a bright spot, until paralysis of some of the brain centers supervenes, and in that way he is cast into a condition of perfect passivity, in which it is possible that the lower astral senses may come into a measure of activity. Naturally he has no power of selection in receiving under such circumstances; he must submit himself to whatever comes in his way, good or bad - and on the whole it is much more likely to be bad than good. Sometimes the same general result is obtained by the recitation of certain formulae, the repetition of which over and over again deadens the mental faculty almost as the gazing at a metal disc does. It may be remembered that the poet Tennyson tells us that he was able by the recitation of his own name many times in rapid succession to pass into another condition of consciousness. The account is given in a letter in the poet's handwriting, which is dated Faringford, Freshwater, Isle of Wight, May 7th, 1874. It was written to a gentleman who communicated to him certain strange experiences he had when passing from under the effect of anesthetics. Tennyson says:

"I have never had any revelations through anesthetics; but a kind of waking trance (this for lack of a better name) I have frequently had, quite up from boyhood, when I have been all alone. This has often come upon me through repeating my own name to myself silently, till all at once out of the intensity of the consciousness of individuality, the individuality itself seemed to dissolve and fade away into boundless being; and this not a confused state, but the

clearest of the clearest, the surest of the surest, utterly beyond words, where death was an almost laughable impossibility, the loss of personality (if so it were) seeming no extinction, but the only true life. I am ashamed of my feeble description. Have I not said the state is utterly beyond words? This is the most emphatic declaration that the spirit of the writer is capable of transferring itself into another state of existence, is not only real, clear, simple, but that it is also infinite in vision and eternal in duration."

Now here is undoubtedly a touch of the higher life; no one who has practical experience of realities can fail to recognize the description as far as it goes, even though the poet just stops short on the brink of something so infinitely grander. He seems to have held himself more positive than do many people who dabble in these matters without the necessary instruction or knowledge, and so he gained a valuable certainty of the existence of the soul apart from the body; yet even his method cannot be commended as good or really safe.

We are sometimes told that such a faculty can be developed by means of exercises, which regulate the breathing, and that this plan is one largely adopted and recommended in India. It is true that a type of clairvoyance may be developed along these lines, but too often at the cost of ruin both physical and mental. Many attempts of this sort have been made here in the United States; I know it personally, because on my previous visit many who had ruined their constitutions and in some cases brought themselves to the verge of insanity came to me to know how they could be cured. Some have succeeded in opening astral vision sufficiently to feel themselves perpetually haunted; some have not even reached that point, yet have wrecked their physical health or weakened their minds so that they are in utter despair; some one or two declare that such practice has been beneficial to them. It is true that such exercises are employed in India by the Hatha Yogis - those who attempt to attain development rather by physical means than by inner growth of the mental and the spiritual. But even among them such practices are used only under the direct orders of responsible teachers, who watch the effect upon the pupil of what is prescribed, and will at once stop him if the exercises prove unsuitable for him. But for people who know nothing at all of the subject to attempt such things indiscriminately is most unwise and dangerous, for practices which are useful for one man may very well be disastrous for another. They may suit one man in fifty, but they are extremely likely not to suit the rest, and myself I should advise every one to abstain from them unless directed to try them by a competent teacher who really understands what they are intended to achieve. You may be the one man whom they will suit, but the probabilities are against it, for there are far more failures than successes. It is so fatally easy to do a great deal of harm in this way, that to experiment vaguely is rather like going into a chemist's shop and taking down drugs at random; you might happen to hit upon exactly what you needed, but also you might not, and the latter is many times more probable.

Another method by which clairvoyance may be developed is by mesmerism - that is to say, if a person be thrown by another into a mesmeric trance, it is possible that in that trance he may see astrally. The mesmerizer entirely dominates his will, and the physical faculties are thrown utterly into abeyance. That leaves the field open, and the mesmerist can at the same time stimulate the astral senses by pouring vitality into the astral body. Good results have been produced in this way, but it requires a very unusual combination of circumstances, an almost superhuman development of purity in thought and intention both in the operator and the subject to make the experiment a safe one. The mesmerist gains great influence over his subject - a far greater power than is generally known: and it may be unconsciously exercised. Any quality of heart or mind possessed by the mesmerist is very readily transferred to the subject, so if he be not entirely pure, we see at once that avenues of danger open up before us. To be thrown into a trance is to give up your individuality, and that is never a good thing in psychic experiments; but beyond and above that element of undesirability there is real danger unless you have the highest purity of thought, word and deed in your operator; and how rarely that is to be found you know as well as I do. I should never myself submit to this process; I should never advise it to any one else.

I say nothing against the practice of curative mesmerism by those who understand it; that is a totally different matter, for in that it is unnecessary to produce the trance condition at all. It is perfectly possible to relieve pain, to remove disease, or to pour vitality into a man by magnetic passes, without "putting him to sleep" at all. To this there can be no possible objection; yet the man who tries to do even this much would do well to acquaint himself thoroughly with the literature of the subject, for there must always remain a certain element of danger in playing, even with the noblest intentions, with forces which you do not understand, which to you are still abnormal forces. None of these are plans of clairvoyant development, which can be unreservedly recommended for trial by every one.

What, then, it may be asked, are the desirable methods, since so many are undesirable? Broadly, those which instead of suppressing the physical body by force, train the soul to control it. The surest and safest way of all is to put oneself into the hands of a competent teacher, and practice only what he advises. But where is the qualified teacher to be found? Not, assuredly among any who advertise themselves as teachers; not among those who take money for their instruction, and offer to sell the mysteries of the universe for so many shillings or so many dollars. Knowledge can be gained now where it has always been available - at the hands of those who are adepts in this great science of the soul, the fringe of which we are beginning to touch in our deepest studies. There has always been a great Brotherhood of the men who know, and they have always been ready to teach their lore to the right man, for it is for that very purpose that they have taken the trouble to acquire it, in order that they may be able to guide and help. How can we reach them? You cannot reach them in the physical body, and you might not even know them if it should happen to you to see them. But they can reach you, and assuredly they will reach you when they see you to be fit for the work of helping the world. Their one great interest is the furthering of evolution, the helping of humanity; they need men devoted to this work, and they are ever watching for them; so none need fear that he can be overlooked if he is ready for that work. They will never gratify mere curiosity; they will give no aid to the man who wishes to gain powers for himself alone; but when a man has shown by long and careful training of himself, and by using for helpfulness all the power that he already possesses, that his will is strong enough and his heart pure enough to bear his part in the divine work - then he may become conscious of their presence and their aid when he least expects it.

It is true that they founded the Theosophical Society, yet membership in the Society will not of itself be sufficient to bring a man into relationship with them - no, nor even membership in that inner School through which the Society offers training to its more earnest members. It is true that from the ranks of the Society men have been chosen to come into closer relation with them; but none could guarantee that as a result of becoming a member, for it rests with them alone, for they see further into the hearts of men than we. But always be sure of this, you whose hearts are yearning for the higher life, for something greater than this lower world can give, that they never overlook one honest effort, but always recognize it by giving through their pupils such teaching and such help as the man at his stage is ready for.

In the meantime, while you are trying in every way to develop yourselves along the path of progress, there is much that you can do, if you wish, to bring this power of clairvoyance nearer within your reach. Remember that it is not in itself a sign of great development; it is only one of the signs, for man has to advance along many lines simultaneously before he can reach his goal of perfection. See how highly developed is the intellect in the great scientific man; yet perhaps he may have but little yet of the wonderful force which devotion gives. See the splendid devotion of the great saint of some Church or religion; yet in spite of all that progress along one line he may have but little yet of the divine power of the intellect. Each needs what the other has, each will have to acquire the faculty of the other before he will be perfect, So it is evident that at present we are unequally developed! Some have more in one direction, and some in another, according to the line along which each has worked most in past lives. So if you particularly long for devotion in your character, by striving in that direction now you may attain much of it even in this life, and may assuredly make it a leading quality in your next life. So with intellect, so with every quality; so also with this faculty of clairvoyance. If you think it well to throw your strength into work along this line, you may do very much towards bringing these latent faculties into action. I am not speaking here of a vague possibility, but of a definite fact, for some of our own members in this Society set themselves years ago to try to train the soul along the path of permanent progress, and of those who persevered without faltering almost every one has even already found some definite result. Some have won their faculties fully, others only partially as yet, but in all cases good has come from their efforts to take themselves in hand and control their minds and emotions.

If you have this desire for higher sight, take yourself in hand first in the same way; make sure first of the mental and moral development, lest you should succeed in your efforts, and gain your powers. For to possess them without having first acquired those other qualifications would be indeed a curse and not a blessing, for you would then misuse them, and your last state would indeed be worse than the first. If you consider that you have made sure of yourself, and you can trust yourself under all possible circumstances to do the right for the right's sake, even against your earthly seeming interest, always to choose the utterly unselfish course of action, and to forget yourself in your love for the world, then there are at least two methods which will leads you towards clairvoyance safely, and can in no way do you harm, even though you should not succeed in your object. The first of these, though perfectly harmless and even useful, is not suited for every one, but the second is of universal application, and I have myself known both of them to be successful.

This first method is a purely intellectual one, a study to which I have already on several occasions had to refer, the study of the Fourth Dimension of space. The physical brain has never been accustomed to act at all along those lines, and so it feels itself unable to attack such a problem. But the brain, like any other part of the physical organism, can be trained by persistent, gradual, careful effort to feats which appeared originally quite beyond its reach, and so it can be induced to understand and conceive clearly the forms of a world unlike its own. The chief apostle of the Fourth Dimension is Mr. C. H. Hinton, of Washington, D.C. He is not a member of our Society, but he has done many of its members an excellent piece of service in writing so clearly and luminously on his wonderful subject. In his books he tells us that he has himself succeeded in developing this power of higher conception in the physical brain, and several of our own members have followed in his footsteps. One of these has developed astral sight simply by steadily raising the capacity of the physical brain until it contained the possibility of grasping astral form, and thus awakening the latent astral faculty proper. It is simply a question of extending the power of receptivity until it includes the astral matter. But I suppose that out of a score of men who took up this study, not more than one would succeed as well and as quickly as that; but at any rate the study is a most fascinating one for those who have a mathematical turn of mind, and where it does not bring increased faculty to see, it must at least bring wider comprehension and a broader outlook over the world, and this is no mean result, even if no other be attained. Short of absolute astral sight, it is the only method of which I know by which a clear comprehension can be gained of the appearance of astral objects, and thus a definite idea of what the astral life really is.

If that line of effort commends itself only to the few, our second method is of universal application. It also is not easy, but its practice cannot but be of the greatest use to the man. That is its great and crowning advantage; it leads a man towards these powers which he so ardently desires; but the rate at which he can move along that road depends upon the degree of his previous development in that particular way in other lives, and therefore no one can guarantee him a certain result in a certain time; yet while he is working his way onward, every step which he takes is so far an improvement, and even though he should work for the whole of his life without winning astral sight, he would nevertheless be mentally and morally and even physically the better for having tried. This is what in various religions is called the method of meditation. For the purpose of our examination of it I shall divide it into three successive steps: concentration, meditation and contemplation, and I will explain what I mean by each of these three terms.

But remember always that to attain success, this effort must be only one side of a general development, and that it is absolutely prerequisite for the man who would learn its secrets to live a pure and altruistic life. There is no secret about the rules of the greater progress, the Steps of the Path of Holiness have been known to the world for ages, and in my little book "Invisible Helpers" I have given a list of them according to the teaching of the Buddha, with the characteristics which mark each of its stages. There is no difficulty in knowing what to do, the difficulty is in carrying out the directions which all religions have given.

The first step necessary towards the attainment of the higher clairvoyance is concentration - not to gaze at a bright spot until you have no mind left, but to acquire such control over your mind that you can do with it what you will, and fix it exactly where you want to hold it for as long a period as you choose. This is not an easy task, it is one of the most difficult and arduous known to man, but it can be done, because it has been done - not once, but hundreds of times, by those whose will is strong and immovable. There may be some among us who have never thought how much beyond our control our minds usually are. Stop yourself suddenly when you are walking along the street, or when you are riding in the car, and see what you are thinking, and why. Try to follow the thought back to its genesis, and you will probably be surprised to find how many desultory thoughts have wandered through your brain during the previous five minutes, just dropping in and dropping out again and leaving almost no impression. You will gradually begin to realize that in truth all these are not your thoughts at all, but simply cast-off fragments of other people's thoughts. The fact is that thought is force, and every exertion of it leaves an impression behind. A strong thought about some other person goes to him, a strong thought of self clings about the thinker; but so many thoughts are not by any means strong or especially pointed in any direction, and so the forms which they create are vaguely-floating and evanescent. While they last they are capable of entering into any mind that happens to come their way, and so it comes that as we walk along the road we leave a trail of feeble thought behind us, and the next man who passes that way finds these valueless fragments intruding themselves upon his consciousness. They drift into his mind, unless it is already occupied with something definite, and in the majority of cases they just drift out again, having made only the most trifling impression upon his brain; but here and there he encounters one which interests or pleases him and then he takes that up and turns it over in his mind, so that it departs from him somewhat strengthened by the addition of a little of his mind-force to it. He has made it his own thought for a moment, and so has colored it with his personality. Every time we enter a room we step into the midst of a crowd of thoughts, good, bad or indifferent as the case may be, but the great mass of them just a dull, purposeless fog, which is hardly worth calling thought at all.

If we wish to develop any higher faculty, we must begin by gaining control over this mind of ours. We must give it some work to do, instead of just letting it play about as it will, drawing into itself all those thoughts which are not ours, which we really do not want at all. It must be not our master but our servant before we can take the first step along the line of the true trained clairvoyance, for this is the instrument, which we shall have to use, and it must be at our command and fully under our control.

This concentration is one of the hardest things for the ordinary man to do, because he has had no practice at it, and indeed has scarcely realized that it needed to be done. Think what it would be if your hand were as little under your control as your mind is, if it did not obey your command, but started aside from what you wished it to do. You would feel that you had paralysis, and that your hand was useless. But if you cannot control your mind, that is dangerously like a mental paralysis; you must practice with it until you have it in hand and can use it as you wish. Fortunately concentration can be practiced all day long, in the common affairs of everyday life. Whatever you are doing, do it thoroughly, and keep your mind on it. If you are writing a letter, think of your letter and of nothing else until it is finished; it will be all the better written for such care. If you are reading a book, fix your mind on it and try to grasp the author's full meaning. Know always what you are thinking about, and why; keep your mind at intelligent work, and do not leave it time to be so idle, for it is in those idle moments that all evil comes.

Even now you can concentrate very perfectly when your interest is sufficiently keenly excited. Then your mind is so entirely absorbed that you hardly hear what is said to you or see what passes round you. There is a story told in the East about some skeptical courtiers, who declined to believe that an ascetic could ever be so occupied with his meditation as to be unaware that an army passed close by him as he sat under his tree wrapped in thought. The king, who was present, assured them that he would prove to them the possibility of this, and proceeded to do so in a truly Oriental and autocratic way. He ordered that some large water-jars should be brought and filled to the brim. Then he instructed the courtiers each to take one and carry it; and his command was that they should walk, carrying this water, through the principal streets of the city. But they were to be surrounded by his guards with drawn swords, and if one of them spilled one single drop of his water, that unfortunate was to be instantly beheaded then and there. The courtiers started on their journey filled with terror; but they all got safely back again, and the king smilingly greeted them with a request to tell him all the incidents of their walk, and describe the persons whom they had met. Not one of them could mention even one person that they had seen, for all agreed that they had been so entirely occupied with the one idea of watching the brimming jars that they had noticed nothing else of any sort. "So, gentlemen", rejoined the king, "you see that when there is sufficient interest concentration is possible."

When you have attained concentration such as that, not under the stress of the fear of instant death, but by the exertion of your will, then you may profitably try the next stage of effort.

I do not say that it will be easy, on the contrary, it is very difficult; but it can be done, for many of us have had to do it. When your mind is thus an instrument, try what we call meditation. Choose a certain fixed time for yourself, when you can be undisturbed; the early morning is in many ways the best, if that can be managed. It is not always an easy time for us now, for we have in modern civilization hopelessly disarranged our day, so that noon is no longer its middle point, as it should be. Now we lie in bed long after the sun has risen, and then stay up injuring our eyes with artificial light long after he has set at night. But choose your time, and let it be the same time each day, and let no day pass without your regular effort. You know if you are trying any sort of physical exercise for training purposes how much more effective it is to do a little regularly than to make a violent effort one day, and then do nothing for a week. So in this matter it is the regularity that is important.

Sit down comfortably where you will not be disturbed, and, turn your mind, with all its newly-developed power of concentration upon some selected subject demanding high and useful thought. We in our Theosophical studies have no lack of such subjects, combining deepest interest with greater profit. If you prefer it, you can take some moral quality, as is advised by the Catholic Church when it prescribes this exercise. In that case, you would turn the quality over in your mind, see how it was an essential quality in the Divine order, how it was manifested in Nature about you, how it had been shown forth by great men of old, how you yourself could manifest it in daily life, how (*perhaps*) you have failed to display it in the past, and so on. Such meditation upon a high moral quality is a very good exercise in many ways, for it not only trains the mind but keeps the good thought constantly before you. But it needs to be preceded generally by thought upon concrete subjects, and when those are easy for you, you can usefully take up the more abstract ideas.

When this has become an established habit with you, with which nothing is allowed to interfere; when you can manage it fairly well without any feeling of strain or difficulty, and without a single wandering thought venturing to intrude itself; then you may turn to the third stage of our effort - contemplation. But remember that you will not succeed with this until you have entirely conquered the mind-wandering. For a long time you will find, when you try to meditate, that your thoughts are continually going off at a tangent, and you do not know it till suddenly you start to find how far away they have gone. You must not let this dishearten you, for it is the common experience; you must simply bring the errant mind back again to its duty, a hundred or a thousand times if necessary, for the only way to succeed is to decline to admit the possibility of failure. But when you have at length succeeded, and the mind is definitely mastered, then we reach that for which all the rest has been but the necessary preparation, good though it has also been in itself.

Instead of turning over a quality in your mind, take the highest spiritual ideal that you know. It does not matter what it is, or by what name you call it. A Theosophist would most probably take one of those Great Ones to whom we have already referred - a member of that great Brotherhood of

Adepts, whom we call the Masters - especially if he had the privilege of having come directly into contact with one of them. The Catholic might take the Blessed Virgin or some patron saint; the ordinary Christian would probably take the Christ; the Hindu would perhaps choose Krishna, and the Buddhist most likely the Lord Buddha himself. Names do not matter, for we are dealing with realities now. But it must be to you the highest, that which will evoke in you the greatest feeling of reverence, love and devotion that you are capable of experiencing. In place of your previous meditation, call up the most vivid mental image that you can make of this ideal, and, letting your most intense feeling go out towards this highest One, try with all the strength of your nature to raise yourself towards Him, to become one with Him, to be in and of that glory and beauty. If you will do that, if you will thus steadily continue to raise your consciousness, there will come a time when you will suddenly find that you are one with that ideal as you never were before, when you realize and understand Him as you never did before, for a new and wonderful light has somehow dawned for you, and all the world is changed, for now for the first time you know what it is to live, and all life before seems like darkness and death to you as compared with this.

Then it will all slip away again, and you will return to the light of common day - and darkness indeed will it appear by comparison! But go on working at your contemplation, and presently that glorious moment will come again and yet again; and each time it will stay with you longer, till there comes a period when that higher life is yours always, no longer a flash or a glimpse of paradise, but a steady glow, a new and never-ceasing marvel every day of your existence. Then for you day and night will be one continuous consciousness, one beautiful life of happy work for the helping of others; yet this, which seems so indescribable and so unsurpassable, is only the beginning of the entrance into the heritage in store for you and for every child of man. Look about you with that new and higher sight, and you will see and grasp many things which until now you have never even suspected - unless, indeed you have previously familiarized yourself with the investigations of your predecessors along this path.

Continue your efforts, and you will rise higher still, and in due course there will open before your astonished eyes a life as much grander than the astral as that is than the physical, and once more you will feel that the true life has been unknown to you until now; for all the while you are rising nearer to the One life which alone is perfect Truth and perfect Beauty.

This is a development that must take years, you will say. Yes, that is probable, for you are trying to compress into one life the evolution, which would normally spread itself over many; but it is far more than worth the time and the effort. No man can say how long it will take in any individual case, for that depends upon two things - the amount of crust that there is to break through, and the energy and determination that is put into the work. He could not promise you that in so many years you would certainly succeed; he can only tell you that many have tried before you, and that many have succeeded. All the great Masters of Wisdom were once men at our own level; as they have risen, so must we rise. Many of us in our humbler way have tried also, and have succeeded, some more and some less, but none who has tried regrets his attempt, for whatever he has gained, be it little or much, is gained for all eternity since it inheres in the soul which survives death. Whatever we gain thus we possess, in full power and consciousness, and have it always at our command; for this is no mediumship, no feeble intermittent trance-quality, but the power of the developed and glorified life which is to be that of all humanity some day.

But the man who wishes to try to unfold these faculties within himself will be very ill-advised if he does not take care first of all to have utter purity of heart and soul, for that is the first and greatest necessity. If he is to do this, and to do it well, he must purify the mental, the astral and the physical; he must cast aside his pet vices and his physical impurities; he must cease to defile his body with meat, with alcohol or tobacco, and try to make himself pure and clean all through, on this lower plane as well as on the higher ones. If he does not think it worth giving up petty uncleanness for the higher life, that is exclusively his own affair; it was said of old that one could not serve God and Mammon simultaneously. I do not say that bad habits on the physical plane will prevent him altogether from any psychic development, but do very emphatically and distinctly say that the man who remains unclean is never free from danger, and that to touch holy things with impure hands is to risk a terrible peril. The man who would try for the higher must free his mind from worry and from lower cares; while doing his duty to the uttermost, he must do it impersonally and for the right's sake, and leave the result in the hands of higher powers. So will he draw round him pure and helpful entities as he moves onward, and will himself radiate sunlight on those in suffering or in sorrow. So shall he remain master of himself, pure and clean and unselfish, using his new powers never for a personal end, but ever for the advancement and the succor of men his brothers, that they also, as they can, may learn to live the wider life, may learn to rise from amid the mists of ignorance and selfishness into the glorious sunlight of the peace of God.

PSYCHIC AND SPIRITUAL DEVELOPMENT

By Annie Besant

To speak properly, the title of my lecture should be *Psychic Development and Spiritual Unfolding*. That would have made rather too long a title, and yet the difference between the words *development* and *unfolding* is a very important one. When we are dealing with the Spirit we cannot accurately speak of *development*. A Spirit neither develops nor evolves; he only unfolds into manifestation that which eternally lies within him. A Spirit, being identical with the Universal Consciousness, can neither increase nor diminish. What he can do, entering into conditions of time and space, is to turn outwards that which is within, to turn attention outwards, and slowly to conquer, by this contact with matter, that knowledge of the universe regarded as phenomenal, which does not come into his consciousness when he is separated off from the universal by that delicate film of matter which is his vehicle in the nirvanic, or spiritual, sphere. Within that seed of Divinity all possibilities are contained. It is only the turning outwards which is possible, by the contact with the various planes of matter.

On the other hand, with regard to psychic development, which depends entirely on the conditions of the matter which veils the Spirit, the word *development* is entirely accurate. Psychic progress is literally the evolving and developing of form after form, the forms being separate the one from the other, and being, as regards three of them, new-born at each birth, and dying one after the other in the process of death and of after-death. So that we are face to face with two entirely different processes, which I propose to try to make rather more clear than they are in the minds of many.

These two things are fundamentally different in nature. They belong to those two great opposites by the interaction of which the universe is built — Spirit and Matter. You cannot have two things more absolutely opposed. You may reach that which is Spirit by denying one after the other all the qualities and manifestations of matter. There ought, then, to be a very wide gulf in the minds of students with regard to that which belongs to the development of the psychic, and that which belongs to the unfolding of the Spirit, and if we can get rid of the confusion that exists so largely amongst us we shall not have wasted time.

Let us glance first at the spiritual and ask what it is. Carry your mind to the higher or spiritual Triad, that reproduction of the Monad as Spirit in his threefold nature, as Will, Intuition and Intellect, sometimes called Atma-buddhi-manas. The Monad himself is the essence and root of Spirit, the Spirit being his reproduction in the three higher spheres of our fivefold system, showing out his three aspects of Power, Wisdom and Activity; these are manifested by the ray of the Monad appropriating an atom from each of the three spheres, the spiritual, intuitional and intellectual; these condition the manifestation of the monad, each variety of matter showing forth one aspect only, as though the three aspects were separable. Not one of these really exists in separation; where Spirit shows himself forth as Will in the spiritual sphere, there are also present, though subordinate, the two aspects of the Monad which appear in the two succeeding spheres, Intuition and Intellect; both are present in that atmic particle, and form part of its consciousness, although dominated by that Will by which Atma shows himself forth. So again when you take the second aspect, showing itself forth as Intuition (Buddhi), you cannot separate off from that either Will (Atma) or Intellect (Manas); they are both implicitly present, although it is the Wisdom aspect of the Monad which is there dominant. And so with the third. When we come to intellect, showing forth the active, or creative aspect of the Monad, there also we have to recognize the implicit presence of Will and Intuition. Consciousness is one, and it can never show out one aspect alone without the other two being present. You will find it is laid down by one of the greatest of Indian psychologists, that we have here continually a reflection and a re-reflection within the Self and that when we speak of one of them we are thinking of that aspect as working upon itself, and so showing forth that quality predominantly; but that in that same sphere we have the other two aspects, colored indeed, as it were, by the first; in each case all three are present, two as reflected on to the third, that third dominating the two reflections. And in this way is made up a ninefold division, giving a marvelously accurate classification. But for us just now it is enough to recognize one dominant aspect and two others implicitly present.

When we come down from those two and a half higher spheres, where the true spiritual Triad shows itself forth, to the lower two and a half spheres we come into the world where matter is dominant. In the higher, consciousness prevails, over matter. In the lower, matter prevails over consciousness. The division of higher and lower comes in the middle of the mental sphere, so that the three sub-planes belong to the world of Spirit predominantly, the lower four belonging predominantly to the world of phenomena. In the lower spheres the matter which veils the Spirit, conditions it far more forcibly and obviously than does the matter on the higher; and the work of the Spirit on those lower planes will be the molding and organizing of matter, in the effort to create for himself vehicles which will express him in the lower world, and deprive him as little as possible of his own inherent powers.

In that lower world also you will see this same triplicity of manifestation continually showing forth, though there again one aspect predominates over the others. For instance, in the emotional sphere, the astral body serves for the vehicle of activity and thought as well as for the vehicle of emotion, and the man working in the astral sphere is the same man as the man working here, with none of his consciousness lost, and showing out the three faces, as they also show out here in the physical body. There is always a danger, as we analyze man into factors, of losing sight of this unit nature of consciousness. When we are dealing with the physical body we recognize the aspects of consciousness and their places of manifestation; we understand quite well that the mental aspect works through the cerebro-spinal nerves, the emotional through the sympathetic system and glands, the volitional through the muscles; all are present. We must do the same with the astral and mental spheres. This close study of consciousness and its vehicles is absolutely necessary for a real understanding of Spirituality and Psychism.

When we study the spiritual, we are dealing with consciousness in the higher spheres, the characteristic mark of which is unity. *He,* says Shri Krishna, "who seeth Me in all things, and all things in Me, he seeth, verily he seeth". Nothing other than that is spiritual vision. There is no vision entitled to be called spiritual, save that which sees God in Nature and Nature in God, which recognizes the One Universal Bliss, the One Universal Self-Consciousness, the One Universal Existence, and sees all things rooted in THAT and in THAT alone. To realize the Self-Consciousness is alone Wisdom. And we must bear clearly in mind this definition of the Spirit, that it is the consciousness of Unity, of Oneness with the Supreme. Again it is written: "There is nothing moving or unmoving that can exist bereft of Me". That is everywhere to be seen and, recognized, and none may call himself spiritual if he does not to some extent enjoy that realization of the Oneness.

Spirituality is an exceedingly different thing from Psychism, which is the manifestation of Intellect, cognizing the external worlds, and seeing the differences, the diversity, in all those worlds. It does not matter whether you are looking at physical, astral, or mental objects; all looking at objects, all the activity of consciousness utilizing matter as a means of contact with objects, is covered by the word Psychism. It depends for its development on the organization of the sheaths, on their delicacy and refinement; and for the purpose of understanding this, it is enough to think of the human being as composed of consciousness and matter, taking the three lower sheaths simply as the sense-garment. Drop for a moment the thought of the physical, astral, and mental *bodies* the word *body* seems to connote too much of difference; they are only matter at different stages of density, and the three together make up the sense-garment of the consciousness, Throughout the psychic development, the improvement of the sense-garment is the task which the student has before him; He wants to make each layer of the sense-garment more refined, more sensitive, and to realize it more and more clearly as a garment and not as himself — one garment in three layers. All the evolution that goes on in that garment improves psychic development, bringing the mind into fuller touch with the external world.

If that be clearly grasped, you cannot confuse the psychic and the spiritual, for one belongs wholly to the consciousness in its unity, and the other to the sense-garment in its multiplicity. And you will be inclined neither to overvalue nor to undervalue psychic development. Students are inclined to run into extremes. Neither extreme position is true. One should take the common-sense view of what is called *psychism*. Psychism is the manifestation of consciousness through its sense-garment, and everything that increases the translucency of that garment, in one or other of these layers, is part of psychic development. In our present stage of evolution a large part of this psychic development is going on in the astral body. Consciousness has largely conquered the physical layer of the sense-garment in most people, and is beginning to conquer the astral layer; but as that progress is at present abnormal, it is regarded as something almost supernatural, instead of being taken in the same quiet common-sense way that you take the higher orders of the physical senses amongst ourselves. We know the good musician has a much more delicate ear than most of us, but we do not look on him as apart from us because of that. Taking that delicacy a little further and carrying it to the next layer of the sense-garment does not alter its quality. It is a question of degree and not of kind.

In the physical part of the garment, the lowest layer of the body, there is a sharper division between the senses than there is in other layers. In the mental sphere the consciousness which has not yet touched the physical has a keen recognition of the life within an object, and a very confused impression of the garment of matter in which that consciousness is veiled, the garment which makes it an object. So also, coming down into the emotional, or astral sphere, if you take a consciousness that has had no experience of the physical plane at all (as in the Elemental Kingdom) you will find that the entities do not receive from the astral object the clearly defined outline, but a far more blended impression. There are no sharp lines of distinction between the senses; hearing and sight, for instance, melt into one another. It is true that you can point to one part and say: *that is sight*, and to another: *that is hearing*, but you come to a place where you cannot distinguish clearly between the two senses, for that clear definition takes place for the first time on the physical plane. Only consciousness, having once obtained that definition, does not lose it when it is active in the second layer of the sense-garment. It keeps the definition, and that is what is gained from the physical body, even when the physical body is finally thrown off. Consciousness having passed

39

through the physical sphere never again loses that clearness and definiteness which in the physical sphere it gained. So that when you come to the psychic evolution in the second layer, the astral, you find the advantage of the consciousness having passed through the physical stage.

There is another phrase that comes into my mind from the great Scripture I have already quoted: *without senses enjoying sense objects* — a phrase which sounds extremely strange and rather unintelligible. The reason is the one I have just spoken of, that the clear definition of the powers of perception in the consciousness is not dependent on the organs, after the organs have served their purpose and have given to it the necessary definition. It is said even of the LOGOS Himself, who is spoken of in that verse; having passed through all these experiences, He has carried with Him to that lofty rank of Divinity the qualities which in the humbler days of earth, in far-off universes, He slowly gathered and built into Himself as we are building them now.

The whole of the development of consciousness in the sense-garment is psychic, whether in one layer or another. You should not limit the word to the astral and mental spheres, for by making a difference of term in that way you lose the sense of the unity of evolution.

The evolution of the astral body largely takes place from the mental sphere, as the organization of the physical senses and their apparatus takes place from the astral sphere. As you are working in the developing of your mind now, that mind, in its more evolved stage, fashions for itself that astral layer of the sense-garment which it will be able to use more independently as evolution proceeds. And to develop healthily that second layer, it must be developed from above and not from below. It is possible to stimulate the growth of the sense-organs in the astral body to some extent from the physical senses, but such stimulation does not carry us very far. Also, it has the tendency to injure the physical organs used, and what is more serious, to injure in the brain those particular centers which, in the later evolution of the astral senses, would be their proper points of expression on the physical plane. For within our brain are certain centers which are the places of junction between the astral and physical sense-organs, making possible the bringing down of the information gathered by the astral into the physical consciousness working through the brain. Suppose the astral chakra; which answers to astral sight, is active. That has its corresponding point between the eyebrows, and a certain development of a center in the physical body between the eyebrows goes on as the result of the development of that astral sense in the astral body. It is that which lies at the root of the practice of some people in psychometry, and a little-developed form of clairvoyance, where they sometimes put an object to the forehead when trying to psychometrise, or to see with the astral sight. That particular center and the solar plexus are the two chief centers in making a link of connection between the astral and physical layers of the sense-garment. But if, instead of stimulating from the physical, you stimulate from the mental, then your astral centers develop healthily and naturally, and with that will come, without any very special effort, the descent of the information gathered in that second layer into the first, so that you become consciously *clairvoyant, clairaudient,* and so on.

When those faculties appear in the waking consciousness the person is called a *psychic* or a *sensitive;* and the name means nothing more than this: that there is a beginning of the shaping of those senses, and that the links between the two layers of the sense-garment are beginning to work. It is a great advantage for the gaining of knowledge to have the astral senses as well as the physical at your disposal; but it will only give you more phenomenal knowledge; it will not quicken your spiritual unfolding. Nay, it may possibly delay it, because it makes the phenomenal more attractive than before. It is more difficult for the person in whom these finer senses are developed to turn away from the outer and more attractive phenomena, and to fix the attention inwards to evoke the true spiritual vision, the knowledge of the One.

It is for that reason that in many of the ancient books — whether Indian, Grecian, or Egyptian — you find so little stress laid on the development of these higher sensuous powers. It is seen that sometimes the person in whom they are developed is thereby made more separate and not more united; whereas in the spiritual unfolding, the spiritual person feels himself more one with every form of life and less separate. In India the siddhis are definitely regarded as having no part in spiritual development, and those who try to develop them are simply looked at in the same light as those who try to develop keener physical sight or hearing.

The training for psychic development and for spiritual unfoldment is quite different. In psychic development you have to deal with the perfection and organization of the sense-garment; when you come to deal with the spiritual, the preparation is intellectual, emotional, and moral. I do not mean, in saying that, that morality as such, or the lower intelligence as such, is spiritual; but they are the necessary preparation for the manifestation of the Spirit in man. The growth of the moral character, of self-sacrifice, self-surrender, willingness to serve, the breaking away — of the sense of separateness — all this is the preparation for spiritual unfolding. And so also with regard to the higher intelligence. It is absolutely necessary for the spiritual manifestation; and everything that tends to purify the intelligence and raise it from the concrete to the abstract is an approach towards the region where the spiritual unfolding will take place. Hence the immense stress laid in all ancient books on the building up of virtue on the one side, and of intelligence on the other; so that within the good man and the reasonable man, the spiritual man might descend and find his habitation. Truly, as it is said in *Light on the Path,* "great though the gulf may be between the good man and the sinner . . . it is immeasurable between the good man and the one on the threshold of Divinity". That is true. It is a difference in *kind* and not only in degree. Hence it is that when you are striving to quicken the evolution of man, so that the Spirit may reveal himself within the garb of matter, so much stress is laid on study and on moral training, not as confusing the two, but the one as being the pathway which makes it possible for the other to manifest. The Spirit cannot manifest in the ignorant or in the immoral man; he is latent within him, and until that preparation is made, spiritual unfoldment and manifestation in the world of forms cannot be.

I know that that puts spiritual unfolding very high, and it may shock some people, because whatever is vague they think is spiritual. But really that is not so. A good emotion does not mean consciousness on the buddhic plane. Emotion is not spirituality, although it is often confused with it. There is an enormous gulf between them. Spirituality is the Self-consciousness, conqueror over matter, not the manifestation distorted and stunted in matter, which is emotion. That truth to some people may seem rather cold. It is, of course, nothing of the kind. It is the most inspiring truth which it is possible to put forward, when a glimpse is caught of what it really means; for there is nothing discouraging in recognizing that we have a long path to travel before reaching the spiritual heights. It would be far more discouraging if the small manifestations of emotion and good feeling we find down here were the limit of the Divine in humanity. That they are very often beautiful, I do not deny; but they are not *the* Beauty: that is something wider, vaster, grander, than you or I at present can even conceive. Surely it is more inspiring to the heart and mind to see far off the dawn of a grandeur that some day we know will be ours, than it is to rest content with the miserable and petty manifestations which are all we are capable of at the present time. The one inspires to ceaseless effort, to unwearied aspiration; the other makes us sit down contentedly, thinking we are almost near the manifestation of God in ourselves. But, as we catch a glimpse of those greater possibilities, as we put our thought of Spirit higher and higher, we become more conscious of a strength within ourselves, which makes us mighty enough to rise above the highest that we can dream. Only we need time and patience, a high ideal, and noble thinking. One thing only is the sign that the Spirit in us is beginning to put forth his powers; the possession of peace, serenity, strength, and broadness of view. Those show the germinating of the divine seed within us; and as we see those qualities grow we cannot say: "I am spiritually developed," but we may dare to say: "My face is turned in the right direction, and I am beginning to tread the Path which leads to the manifestation of the Spirit."

PSYCHIC POWERS

By C. W. Leadbeater

The possession of psychic powers does not necessarily involve high moral character, any more than does the possession of great physical strength. It is quite true that the man who enters the Path of Holiness will presently find such powers developing in him, but it is quite possible to gain many of the powers without the holiness. Powers can be developed by any one who will take the trouble, and a man may learn clairvoyance or mesmerism just as he may learn to play the piano, if he is willing to go through the necessary hard work. It is far better and safer for the vast majority of people to work at the development of character, to try to fit themselves for the Path, and to leave the powers to unfold in due course, as they certainly will. Some people are in too much of a hurry to do this, and set themselves to force the powers sooner. Well, if they are quite certain that they desire them only for the sake of helping others, and that they are wise enough to use them rightly, it may be that no harm will come of it; but it is not easy to be quite certain on these points, and the slightest deflection from the right line will mean disaster.

If a man must try to obtain the powers, there are two ways open to him; of course there are many more than two methods, but I mean that they all fall under two heads-- the temporary and the permanent. The temporary method is to deaden the physical sense in some way-- actively by drugs, by self-hypnotism, or by inducing giddiness, for example, or passively by being mesmerised-- so that the astral senses may come to the surface. The permanent way is to work at the development of the ego, so that he may be able to control the lower vehicles and use them as he wishes.

It is somewhat like controlling a troublesome horse. A man who knows nothing of riding may so stupefy a horse with drugs that he can somehow keep on his back, but that will not in the least enable him to control any other horse. So a man who stupefies his physical body may use his astral senses to some extent, but that will in no way help him to manage another physical body in his next birth. The man who will take the far greater trouble of learning to ride properly can then manage any horse, and the man who develops his ego until it can manage one set of vehicles will be able to control any others that are given to him in future lives. This latter course means real evolution; the other does not necessarily involve anything of the sort. It does not follow that everyone who is on the Path must have psychic powers; they are not absolutely necessary until a certain stage of it is reached.

Short of the real psychic powers there are various other methods by which men endeavor to obtain some of the same results. One of these, for example, is the repetition of invocations. Charms and ceremonies may sometimes produce an effect; it depends upon the way in which they are performed. I have seen a man who was able to answer questions in rather a curious way; he first entranced himself by repeating charms over and over again, and his invocations not only influenced himself, but also attracted nature-spirits who went for the desired information, obtained it and put it into his mind.

Lord Tennyson, by repeating his own name over and over again and drawing his consciousness further and further within himself, raised himself into touch with the ego, and then all this life seemed to him child's play, and death nothing but the entrance into a greater life.

The result of many repetitions may often be to throw oneself into the trance condition; but this is not a training of the ego. Its effects last at most only for one life, whereas the powers which result from real spiritual development reappear in subsequent bodies. The man who entrances himself by the repetition of words or charms may probably return as a medium or at least a mediumistic person in his next life, and it must be remembered that mediumship is not a power, but a condition.

Such repetitions may easily lead on to the coarser physical mediumship (by which I mean the sitting for materialization and sensational phenomena of all sorts) which is frequently injurious to health. I do not know that mere trance-speaking injures the body quite so much, though considering the feebleness of the platitudes which are usually the staple of the communications it might certainly be thought likely to weaken the mind!

Let us consider what it is that is required from a physical medium. When an entity on the astral plane, whether it be a dead man or a nature-spirit, wants to produce any result on dense physical matter-- to play on a piano for example, to cause raps, or to hold a pencil in order to write-- he needs an etheric body through which to work, because astral matter cannot act directly on the lower forms of physical matter, but requires the etheric matter as an intermediary to convey the vibrations from the one to the other-- much in the same way as a fire cannot be lighted with paper and coals alone; the wood is needed as an intermediary, otherwise the paper will all burn away without affecting the coal.

That which constitutes a man a physical medium is a want of cohesion between the etheric and the dense parts of the physical vehicle, so that an astral entity can easily withdraw a good deal of the man's etheric body and use it for his own purposes. Of course he returns it-- in fact its constant tendency is to flow back to the medium, as may be seen from the action of the materialized form-- but still the frequent withdrawal of part of the man's body in this way cannot but cause great disturbance and danger to his health.

The etheric double is the vehicle of vitality, the life-principle, which is perpetually circulating through our bodies; and when any part of our etheric double is withdrawn that life-circulation is checked and its current broken. A terrible drain on vitality is then set up, and that is why the medium is so often in a state of collapse after a séance, and also why so many mediums in the long run become drunkards, having first taken to stimulants in order to satisfy the dreadful craving for support which is caused by this sudden loss of strength.

It can never under any circumstances be a good thing for

the health to be constantly subjected to such a drain as this, even though in some cases the more intelligent and careful "spirits" try to pour strength into their medium after a séance, in order to make up for the loss, and thus support him without absolute breakdown for a much longer period than would otherwise be possible.

In cases of materialization, dense physical matter, probably chiefly in the form of gases or liquids, is frequently borrowed from the body of the medium, who actually decreases temporarily in size and weight; and when it takes place, naturally that is a further source of serious disturbance to all the functions.

Of the mediums with whom I used to have sittings thirty years ago one is now blind, another died a confirmed drunkard, and a third, finding himself menaced apoplexy and paralysis, escaped with his life only by giving up séances altogether.

Another form of materialization is that in which the astral body is temporarily solidified. The ordinary materializing "spirit" takes his material from the medium, because that, being already specialised, is more easily arranged into human form, and more readily condensed and moulded than free ether would be. No one connected with any school of white magic would think it right to interfere with the etheric double of any man in order to produce a materialisation, nor would he disturb his own if he wished to make himself visible at a distance. He would simply condense, and build into and around his astral body a sufficient quantity of the surrounding ether to materialise it, and hold it in that form by an effort of will as long as he needed it.

When part of the etheric double is removed from the physical, as in the case of materialisation of the ordinary kind, a connecting current is visible to any one capable of seeing matter in the etheric condition; but the method of connection with the astral body is entirely different, for nothing in the nature of a cord or current of astral matter joins the two forms. Yet it is difficult to express in terms of this plane the exact nature of the exceeding closeness of the sympathy between them; perhaps the nearest approximation we can get to the idea is that of two instruments tuned to exactly the same pitch, so that whatever note is struck upon one of them instantly evokes a precisely corresponding sound from the other.

There is no harm in using will-power to cure diseases, so long as no money or other consideration is taken for what is done. There are several methods; the simplest is the pouring in of vitality. Nature will cure most diseases if the man can be strengthened and supported while she is left to do her work. This is especially true of the various nervous diseases which are so painfully common at the present day. The rest-cure, which is often advised for them, is quite the best thing that can be suggested, but recovery might often be greatly hastened if vitality were poured into the patient in addition. Any man who has surplus vitality may direct it by his will to a particular person; when he is not doing that, it simply radiates from him in all directions, flowing out principally through the hands. If a man is depleted of strength so that his spleen does not do its work properly, the pouring in of specialised vitality is often of the greatest help to him in keeping the machinery of the body going until he is able to manufacture it for himself.

Many minor diseases can be cured merely by increasing the circulation of the vitality. A headache, for example, is generally due either to a slight congestion of blood, or to a similar congestion of the vital fluid; in either case a clairvoyant who can see the obstruction may deal with it by sending a strong current through the head, and washing away the congested matter. A man who cannot see can also produce this result, but since he does not know exactly where to direct this force he generally wastes a great deal of it.

Sometimes people perform cures by imposing their own magnetic conditions upon others. This is based on the theory (which is quite correct) that all disease is in harmony of some sort, and that if perfect harmony can be restored the disease will disappear. So in this case the person who wishes to effect a cure first raises his own vibrations to the highest degree which is possible for him, fills himself with thoughts of love and health and harmony, and then proceeds to enfold the patient within his aura, the idea being that his own powerful vibrations will overbear these of the patient, and gradually bring him into the same harmonious and healthy condition. This method is often effective, but we must remember that it involves imposing the whole of the personality of the magnetiser upon the patient, which may not always be desirable for either of the persons concerned.

One should take care not to be caught or entangled on the astral plane, as a man easily may be, and that through his virtues as well as his vices, if he be not exceedingly cautious. For example, it is possible to affect others by thought, and thus obtain whatever is wanted from them, and the temptation of this power to an ordinary man would be overwhelming. Again, you could easily *force* those whom you love out of a wrong path into a right one if you wished, but this you must not do; you may only persuade and argue. Here again is a temptation. You may by force prevent your friend from doing wrong, but often the weakening effect of the compulsion on his mind will do him more harm than the wrong-doing from which you save him. Drunkenness can be cured by mesmerising the man, but it is far better to persuade him gradually to conquer the weakness for himself, since this is a thing which he will have to do in some life. It is said that in some cases the man has yielded himself to this awful habit for so long that his will power is entirely in abeyance, and he actually has not the strength to refrain; and it is claimed that for such a man mesmerism is necessary, for it is the only method of giving him an opportunity to reassert himself as a human being, and to regain some sort of control of his vehicles. This may be so, and I can well understand the desire to save by any lawful means the soul which has come to so dire a pass; yet even then I would counsel the greatest care in the use of mesmerism, and in the choice of the mesmerist.

A man can use the faculties of his astral body without moving away from his physical vehicle. That is called the possession of astral powers in the waking state, and is a definite stage in development. But it is more usual for the astral body to leave the physical when it is intended to operate or observe at a distance from the physical body.

The Indian term "sky-walker" generally refers only to one who is able thus to travel in his astral body. But sometimes also it means levitation, in which the physical body is lifted and floats in the air. In India this happens to some ascetics, and some of the greatest of Christian saints have in deep meditation been thus raised from the ground. It involves, however, the expenditure of a good deal of force. When a disciple is commissioned to undertake some special work for humanity, the adepts may give to him for the purpose some extra force, but though he is left free to use it as he pleases, he must not fritter it away uselessly. So it happens that even those who can produce these strange effects at will do not do so to amuse themselves or others, but only for real work. It would be quite possible for some disciple to use this force for the purpose of carrying his physical body through the air to a distant place; but as that would mean a tremendous expenditure of force, it is not likely that he would so use it unless definitely directed to do so.

On the other hand there have been cases in which such powers were used-- for example, to save a man from undeserved suffering. There was once a case in which a young man was accused of the forgery of an important document. He was to a certain extent technically guilty, although quite innocent of any evil intention. He had very foolishly imitated a certain signature upon a blank sheet of paper, and then some one who was unfriendly to him had obtained possession of the sheet of paper, written in certain instructions above the signature, and then cleverly cut the paper so as to make it appear to be a letter conveying orders. The accused had to admit that the signature was in his writing, but his account of the circumstances under which it was written was not unnaturally disbelieved, and it seemed impossible for him to escape the most terrible consequences. But it happened that one of our Masters was called as a witness to testify to the handwriting of the prisoner. The sheet was handed to Him with the question:

"Do you recognise that handwriting as that of the prisoner?"

The Master just glanced at it, and instantly returned it, saying:

"Is this the sheet which you intended to give me?"

In that instant the sheet had become an absolute blank! The counsel for the prosecution of course supposed that in some utterly incomprehensible way he had mislaid the paper; but for want of it the prosecution fell through, and so the young man was saved.

PSYCHISM AND SPIRITUALITY

By Annie Besant

Our subject tonight consists of two words: psychism — spirituality. I am going to speak to you on the subjects denoted by these two words, because there is so much confusion about them in ordinary conversation, in ordinary literature, and out of that confusion much of harm arises. People think of one thing and use the name of the other, and so continually fall into blunders and mislead others with whom they talk. I want tonight to draw a sharp and intelligible division between psychism and spirituality; if possible, to explain very clearly what each of them means; so that, thoroughly understanding the meaning of the things, people may choose for themselves which of the two they desire to evolve, or unfold, within themselves. For if a person, desiring to unfold the spiritual nature, uses the means which are only adapted for developing the psychic nature, disappointment, possibly danger, will result; while, on the other hand, if a person desires to develop the psychic nature, and thinks that he will reach that development quickly by unfolding his spiritual powers, he also is equally doomed to disappointment; but in the second case, only to disappointment for a time. For while it is not true that the great psychic is necessarily a spiritual person, it is true that the great spiritual person is inevitably a psychic. All the powers of Nature are subject to the Spirit, and hence, when a man has truly unfolded his spiritual nature, there is nothing in the lower world which is not open to him and obedient to his will. In that sense, then, the man who follows the spiritual path will not ultimately be disappointed if he is seeking psychic development, but the very seeking for it will, on the spiritual path, act as a certain barrier. I shall return to the point again presently, and show you in what sense, and why, it is true that the development of the psychic powers may hinder the unfolding of the spiritual.

Now, to distinguish clearly between the two, I will begin with two brief definitions. They will be expanded naturally in the course of the lecture, but I will define each of these two words in a single sentence so as to make the definition clear and brief. Spirituality is the self-realisation of the One; psychism is the manifestation of the powers of consciousness through organised matter. Each word of that definition has its own value. We are far too apt, in our ordinary thought and talking, to limit the words "psychical," "psychic," or "psychism" in a quite illegitimate way, and the popular use of the term is illegitimate. It is generally used amongst us to mean unusual manifestations of the powers of consciousness, whereas, properly speaking, the word ought to cover every outer manifestation of consciousness, whether on the physical, on the astral, on the mental, or on the buddhic plane. It does not matter in what world you are moving, in what matter your consciousness is acting; so long as it is utilising organised matter for its own expression so long are those manifestations psychic, and are properly included under the term psychism. You may perhaps wonder why I lay stress on this. You will see it at once if I remind you that unless we keep this definition in mind—accurate, legitimate as it is—we shall be 'making a division between the manifestation of the consciousness on the physical and on the astral and mental planes, between its manifestation in the physical and those in the astral and mental bodies; and if we do that the whole of our thought will be on mistaken lines. You need practically to be pressed back to what you know of consciousness on the physical plane, before you can thoroughly follow its manifestations on the astral and on the mental. If you try to separate off manifestations which are the same in kind though differing in degree, according to the fineness of the matter which is employed, if you try to separate them off, you will always regard what you call psychism—that is, astral and mental manifestations in the subtler bodies—in an artificial and unwise manner. If, on the other hand, you realise that consciousness is one, that its manifestation on any plane is conditioned by the matter of the plane, that it is one in essence, only varying in degree according to the lessening or the increase of the resistance of the matter of the planes, then you will not be inclined to take up exaggerated views with regard to what people are so fond of calling psychism. You will not denounce it in the foolish way of many people, because in denouncing it you will know that you denounce all intellectual manifestations, an absurdity of which very few people are likely to be guilty; if you take your intellectual manifestations in the physical world as admirable things, to be always encouraged, strengthened, developed, then you will be compelled, by parity of reasoning, to understand that the manifestations of the same consciousness in finer matter, astral or mental, are equally worthy, and no more worthy, of development, of consideration. You will not find yourself in the absurdly illogical position of declaring it a good thing to train the physical plane consciousness, while it is dangerous to cultivate the astral and mental plane consciousness. You will understand that all psychism is of the same kind, that on each plane the development of psychism has its own laws ; but that it is absurd to admire the working of consciousness on the lower plane, and shrink from it as something dangerous, almost diabolical, when it appears on a plane higher than the physical.

It is this rational and common-sense view which I want to impress upon you to-night, to get you out of the region of mystery, marvel, wonder, and fear, which to so many people surround what is called psychism; to make you understand that you are unfolding consciousness, showing out your powers on one plane after another according to the organisation and the fineness of the bodies in which your consciousness is working; and that if you will only keep your common sense and reason, if you will only not allow yourself to be terrified by what at present is unusual, you may then walk along the psychic pathway in the astral or mental world, as resolutely, and with as great an absence of hysteria, as walk along the psychic pathway in the physical world. That is the general idea; and, of course, this is the meaning in which, after all, the word is often used down here. When you say "psychology" you do not mean only the workings of consciousness in astral and mental bodies; you mean the whole consciousness of the man, the workings of the mind, wherever the mind is active; the whole of that you include under "psychology." Why, then, when you change its form, should you narrow it down, as though that which is mind on one plane is not also mind on all planes on which the mind is able to function ?

Now let us consider for a moment the workings of the mind on the physical plane: they are familiar. There is, however, one important point about them. In the materialistic science of the last century you had very widely spread, amongst scientific men, the view that thought was only the result of certain kinds of vibration in certain kinds of matter. I need not dwell on that. But you are aware that both in England, and more especially in France and Germany, most elaborate disquisitions were written to prove that thought was only the product of nervous matter. You rarely, I think never, now find a well-trained scientist prepared to commit himself to that position. Those who survive as representatives of that same school may do so, but they are literally survivals. The mass of psychologists of today admit that the manifestations of mind cannot any longer be regarded as the results of vibrations in the physical brain, that at least we must go beyond these limitations when dealing with the results of the study of consciousness, as it is now studied amongst scientific men. They will no longer, then, regard thought as the product of matter. They certainly will not be prepared to go as far as I now propose to go, and say that the thinking organism is the production of thought—the very antithesis, you will agree, of the other position, but which is vital to the understanding of the unfolding of the powers of consciousness through matter. It is recognised in ordinary biology that the function appears before the organ. There I am on safe scientific ground. It is recognised that the exercise of the function gradually builds up the organ. All the researches into the simpler forms of organisms go to prove that. It is also recognised that when the exercise of the function has built the organ in a very simple form, the exercise of the function continually improves the organ which originally it built. So far we are hand in hand with ordinary science. I think I shall not go too far in saying that a large number of the more scientific psychologists of today will at least agree that the brain as you find it in the adult man is very largely the result of the exercise of thinking through the earlier years of life. I do not think they would go so far as to say that thinking has literally produced it. They would, however, judging by very many things that have been said, be willing to admit that by hard thinking we can improve our apparatus of thought. That is one reason for thinking hard—in order to think better. And the harder you think, the more will your thinking instrument improve.

In my next step, however, I cannot by any stretching of ordinary science persuade it to accompany me, or give me a foundation ; for the point is that your consciousness, working on the next plane above the one on which the organ of consciousness is being built, is the shaper of that mechanism. To put it concretely: your physical brain is built up from the astral plane, and it is your consciousness working in matter finer than the physical which builds up the brain in the forming child within the limits laid down by karma. Now, that is a general law for healthy evolution. You will see the importance of this law a little further on. Every body which we possess — physical, astral, mental, buddhic — is always built up by consciousness working in the plane next above it; the next plane, or world, is a world very much more "next" than you are next each other sitting here—not far away beyond the stars, removed by great spaces. It is interpenetrating you in every portion of your being. It is only "next" in the sense that the solids, liquids, and gases of your bodies are next each other in the body—not far away, but here. So that the working is of the closest and most intimate kind. Some of you who are students, of Theosophical literature will remember that H. P. B. has spoken of all of us as working in the astral consciousness. You will see that you are not working with a physical consciousness in the literal sense of the term, if you think for a moment. How much do you know of the consciousness working in the various cells and tissues of your physical body? Practically nothing, except when you are ill. Only when the body is disorganised do you become conscious of that working. Normally, the motion of your blood, the building up by assimilation of your muscles and nerves, the life of your cells, the protective action of some of the living cells in your body—the "devourers," as they are called—go on without your knowledge, without your thought, without your giving one moment's conscious attention to them. In the Perfect Man, the consciousness of all this is ever present, but in us, imperfect, it is not; we are not yet sufficiently vitalised and unfolded to carry on the whole of our consciousness, with full awareness of all its activities. We are only able to manage a very small part of it, and so have let go the consciousness that keeps at work the physical body, to concentrate ourselves in a higher world, and utilise the nervous mechanism as the apparatus of our thinking. That law obtains, then, all through. If you want to organise and build up your astral body, you can only do it from the mental plane. You must raise your thought to a higher power by concentration, by regular meditation, by deliberately working on the consciousness, before you can raise it to that power from which it shall be able to organise your astral body, as it has already organised your physical body. That is the reason why meditation is necessary in all these things; because without the creative power of thought we cannot organise the body in the world which is nearest to the physical.

Now, supposing that we recognise that our consciousness working in the physical brain, the instrument over which we have complete control, is continually at work contacting the outer world, using the brain as an instrument on which it can play, and continually bringing down from higher worlds impressions which it transmits more or less perfectly to the physical plane, we need not dwell upon our ordinary thinking. Let us take thinking a little more unusual, where the finer part of the brain, its etheric matter, is being more largely vitalised, more definitely used. The powers of the imagination—the creative power—the artistic powers, all creative in their nature, these utilise most the ethers of the brain, and, by working in those, bring into activity the lower and coarser matter of the dense brain. Now, the thought passes from the consciousness through vehicle after vehicle to find its clear expression here. But do you not have many mental impressions that are not clear, not well defined, and yet which impress you deeply, and of which you feel sure ? They are of many kinds, and reach you in many ways. What is important to you is simply this for the moment: that being surrounded by the astral and mental worlds, contacts from these are continually touching you, continually causing changes in your consciousness. If your astral body were thoroughly organised like your physical, the impressions made would be clear and sharp like the physical. If your mental body were well organised, the impressions of that plane, the heavenly plane, would be clear and sharp like the physical. But as the astral and mental bodies at this stage of evolution are not well organised, the impressions received by them, causing changes in the consciousness, are vague and indeterminate, and it is these which are generally called "psychic." And when you have a Psychical Research Society, it is not dealing with the ordinary processes of thought, but with those which are not ordinary; and all those things to which it gives many strange names are all workings of the consciousness, in sheaths or bodies of which it has not yet gained the mastery, which it has not yet definitely organised for its purposes. Slowly and gradually they become organised, and strenuous thinking is the method for the astral body, and the working of the pure reason is the method for the mental body. Let us consider with regard to this, whether there is any other way of bringing the astral body and mental body into activity. For you may have noticed that I used the word "normal" evolution, orderly evolution on the lines of natural evolution, always from above. But you may stimulate it from below. It is possible to stimulate the astral body, at least, from the physical plane, but you do it at the cost of higher evolution a little later on, and the reason you can do it is simple enough. In the astral body are all the centres of your senses. You know how after death a man's desires are the same as they were during his physical life. You know how in dreams your desires resemble desires that you may have in your waking consciousness. The centre of all your psychic powers, of your conscious powers, the centres of these are in the astral, and if (especially with your senses, each of which has its own centre in the astral body) you overstrain the physical senses down here, you will get an action on the astral plane, but an unhealthy, because disorderly one, one not going along the line of evolution but trying to create from below instead of from above. None the less, you may have some results, and in the two famous Indian systems for developing the powers of the consciousness, and for unfolding the consciousness itself, you have this recognised, and you read of Raja Yoga and of Hatha Yoga, of the Kingly Yoga and of the Yoga of Effort. The Yoga of Effort is Hatha Yoga, and is practised by physical means and followed by physical effects. The eye is stimulated in certain ways, and the effect of straining the physical eye is to bring about a certain limited kind of clairvoyance. You can gain it in that way by gazing into crystals, and so on. They do stimulate the centre of physical sight, but not the astral; and that is why they cannot go very far. You can get a certain amount of clairvoyance by these means, but you are only expanding your physical sight, and working on centres of the astral body connected with the physical organ of vision, the eye. The true astral sight is an entirely different thing. That comes from a centre of its own in the astral body. It has to be created from the mental body, as the organ of the physical was from the astral. The centre of that sight will be in the mental body and not in the astral, and only the organ of it in the astral body. The method of the Kingly, the Raja Yoga, is always by thought—concentrate, meditate, contemplate, think: by that means, in a healthy, normal, natural way you will inevitably develop the powers of sight on the astral, as in the course of Nature the powers of sight were developed on the physical plane. And if you realise that your consciousness is one, building its bodies for its fuller and more complete expression, that you are here in order to become masters of matter instead of its slaves, to become lords of matter, using every organ of matter for knowledge of the world to which that matter belongs, and not to be blinded by it, as we are for so long a time in our climb upwards, then you will see that this natural development of astral powers is inevitable in the course of evolution, and all that you can do is to quicken it, following the line which Nature has traced. As Nature slowly will evolve in every human being the power of using the astral body as freely as you use the physical body now, so can you quicken the coming of that day for yourselves by understanding the powers of thought and turning them to the object you desire to obtain. There are many ways in which this may be done, and many rules you may learn for your guidance. Those rules may be summed up under two heads: clear and strenuous thinking, discipline for the bodies that you are trying to evolve; and also, I should add, for the body below them in evolution. Those are the two great laws for the safe evolution of these so-called psychic powers, what I call the powers of the consciousness on the astral and mental planes. There must be a discipline for the bodies, for you have to choose the material which will serve you best in the work you are doing out of the innumerable combinations of matter with which Nature presents you. You must choose the combinations that will serve your purpose, which you can utilise in the building of the organs of sense on plane after plane. Just as really as the man who is a drunkard will injure his nervous system by his -excesses, and by supplying coarse and over-active compounds will injure the physical body, so making it a less useful instrument for the man —as any excess, not only drunkenness, but gluttony, profligacy, and so on—as these injure the physical body as an instrument of consciousness, and to have full and perfect consciousness here we must train, discipline, build up our body with knowledge and with self-control, so also is that true on the higher planes. A regimen is necessary when you are dealing with the organisation of the subtler matter of the astral and mental worlds, for you cannot build up your physical body out of the coarser combinations of matter on the physical, and have finer combinations on the astral and mental. The bodies have to match each other. They have to correspond with each other; and as you find all sorts of combinations related the one to the other on every plane, you must choose your combinations on the physical if you desire to choose them also on the astral and mental. You cannot make your physical body coarse, and organise the astral and mental bodies for the finer purposes of the man; and you must settle that in your minds if you wish to try to develop these higher powers of consciousness. Not only because if you gather together the coarser materials of the astral world, you will find yourself hampered by them in the higher expression of consciousness, but also because the presence of these combinations in you exposes you to a number of dangers on the astral plane. The purer the elements of your astral body, the safer you are in your earlier wanderings on that plane. It is important to mention this, because in some of the schools of thought which are trying only to develop astral powers, you will find that they deliberately use other methods in order to make their astral body active. Many schools of the "left hand path" in India will use spirits, wines, meats of all sorts, in order to bring about a certain astral condition, and they succeed, because by these means they attract to themselves, and for a time govern, the elemental powers of those lower planes—the elementals of the lower astral worlds. So that you may find that an Indian, who knows a little of this and wants to use it for his own purposes, will deliberately use these things which are attractive to the elementals of those lower worlds, and gather them around him and use them. But he does it knowing what he does, and aiming at that which he desires to conquer. But amongst those who practise black magic of the higher kinds—of the mental kinds—you have an asceticism as stern and rigid as has ever been used by those who are trying to develop their higher bodies for nobler ends. It is a mistake to think that the brothers of the dark side are, as a rule, licentious and indifferent to what you call morality. On the contrary, they are exceedingly strict. Their faults are the faults of the mind, not the faults of the lower desires, of the organs of the different bodies which may gratify them. Their faults are the more dangerous faults of mental powers misused for personal ends. But they realise very well that if they want the mental powers and the higher ranges of those powers, they must be as rigid in the discipline of the lower bodies as any pupil of the White Lodge could be. Take it, then, that to develop in this way, a regimen for the bodies, as well as the strict working and training of the mind, is absolutely necessary. But with these the result is sure. You cannot set a time for the result, for it depends where the worker is beginning in his present life. In all these matters Nature's laws will not permit of what is called miraculous growth, and if you find persons developing psychic powers very rapidly, when perhaps they have been meditating only a few months, it is because in a previous life they have cultivated these powers and are taking up their lessons again in a more advanced class of evolution, and not in the infant class, as many do in the present life. So that there are differences. Some now beginning are not likely to succeed in their present incarnation; but if that discourages them, one can only say: "If you do not do it now, you will have to begin again next life, and so on and on and on. For Nature's laws cannot be violated, and Nature knows no favoritism and no partiality. Some time or other you have to begin, and the sooner you begin the sooner will you succeed."

Now the whole of this, you will remark, is the training, the organising of bodies. And psychism implies that. You must train, purify, organise, in order that the powers of the consciousness may show forth. You will see very fully now why at the beginning 1 urged you to realise that the whole of these manifestations are similar in kind, so that when you find someone saying to you: "Oh! So-and-so is a psychic," as though that were to condemn the person; "Such-and-such a person is a mere clairvoyant," and so on, as though the fact of possessing clairvoyance were a disadvantage rather than an advantage; then the proper answer is: "Are you prepared to go the whole way with that ?" Many Indians do so (it is the point to which I said I would return); they say that the siddhis, the powers of consciousness manifested on the lower planes, are hindrances to the spiritual life. And so they are in a sense. The spiritual life goes inwards: all psychic powers go outwards. It is the same Self in either case—the Self turning inwards on Itself, or the Self going outwards to the world of objects. But it does not make one scrap of difference whether it goes out to physical, astral, or mental objects: it is all the objective consciousness, and therefore the very reverse of the spiritual. But the Indian does not shrink from that as ordinarily the man in the West does. He is perfectly honest. He says: "Yes, the powers of the intellect applied to the objects of the world are a hindrance in the spiritual life. We do not want them, do not care to think about it. We give up all the objects of the physical plane when seeking the Self." And if you are prepared to say that, then by all means turn aside from psychism, but do not at one and the same time encourage intellectuality on the physical plane and denounce what you call psychism on the others, because that is mere folly. If it is better to be blind here than to see—and the Indian will tell you it often is, because it shuts out all the distracting objects of the physical plane—if you are prepared to say that, and say: "Yes, I would rather be blind than see," then you may go on to denounce seeing on the astral plane. But if you value your physical sight, why not value the astral sight—it is a stage higher—as well ? and the mental sight—which is a stage higher yet—as well ? Why denounce astral and mental, and praise up the physical ? Why admire the power of sight of the painter, who sees more shades than you can see, and denounce the sight of the clairvoyant, who sees very much more than the cleverest painter ? They all belong to the object world ; they all lead the Self away from the realization of himself, and they are all exactly on the same level. It seems strange when one sees the same person exalting the psychic on the physical plane and denouncing it on the astral and mental.

But now let us turn to "spirituality" and see what that means. "The Self-realisation of the One"; not the declaring that all men are one, that all men are brothers: we can all do that. Anyone who has reached a certain stage of intellectual knowledge will recognise the unity of mankind; will say, with the writer in the Christian book, that God has made all men of one blood—quoted again from what is called a Pagan book. That intellectual recognition of the unity is practically universal among educated people; but very few are prepared to carry out the intellectual recognition into practical life and practical training. Now for the development of what are called psychic faculties some amount of retirement from the world is very useful. For the development of the spiritual consciousness no such retirement is necessary. In fact, for the most part, except in the earlier stages perhaps, seclusion is a mistake; for the world is the best place for the unfolding of the sense of unity, and best amongst men and women and children can we call out the powers of the spiritual life. And that for a simple reason. In the lower world the Spirit shows itself out by love, by sympathy; and the more we can love, the more we can sympathise, the greater will be the unfolding of the consciousness of the Self within. It was a true word of the early Christian Initiate, that if a man loves not his brother whom he hath seen, how shall he love God whom he hath not seen? And if the perfection of the spiritual consciousness be that vision of the Supreme, the consciousness which knows itself to be one with God, then the way to the realisation will be by the partial realisation of loving sympathy, for which the world is the most fitting field, and our brethren around us the natural stimulus. Love, sacrifice, these are the manifestations of the Spirit on the physical plane, as is right knowledge also. For the Spirit is not a one-sided thing, but a Trinity, and knowledge is as necessary as love. The special value of love lies in its unifying power, and in the fact that it makes what the world calls sacrifice natural and delightful. You know it in your own experience. Just in proportion as you love another is it a joy and not a sorrow to give up things in order that the happiness of the other may be increased. It is no sacrifice for a mother to give up personal enjoyment for the sake of giving it to her children. A deeper joy is felt in the happiness of the child than could possibly have been felt in the enjoyment of the thing by herself; a sweeter, finer, profounder happiness is the enjoyment of the happiness of the beloved. And that a little widens out the consciousness, and hence family life is one of the best schools for spiritual unfolding ; for in the continual sacrifices of the family life, springing from love and rendered joyful by affection, the Self feels itself a larger Self, and reaches the sense of unity with those immediately around. And after the family the public life, the life of the community, the life of the nation: these also are schools for the unfolding of the spiritual consciousness. For the man who is a good citizen of the community feels the life of the community as his own life, and so becomes conscious of a larger Self than the narrow self of the family. And the man who loves his nation, his Self widens out to the boundaries of the nation, and he is conscious of a larger Self than the self of the family, or the community within the State. And just in proportion as the love widening does not grow superficial and shallow (for if you have only a certain amount of water and you make your dish wider and wider, the water will become shallower and shallower) does it approach spiritual love. Too often love becomes unreal with those who try to love the far-off when they do not love the near. But if you avoid the temptation, and remembering that the Spirit has no limitations, and that you can draw and draw and draw on the love within you and never find the bottom of the source of love; if you are strong enough to do that, then the love of the family, of the community, of the State, will widen out into the love of humanity, and you shall know yourself as one with all, and not only with your family, or your community, or your nation. All these local loves are schoolmasters to bring us to the wider love of man. But do not blunder in the idea that you can have the wider unless you have gone through the narrower; for the bad husband, the bad citizen, the bad patriot, will never make a real lover of humanity. He must learn his alphabet before he can Bead in this book of love, and must spell out the letters before he may pronounce the word. None the less, these successive stages are all stages towards the spiritual life, and prepare the man for the consciously spiritual realisation. And if you would really train yourself for the unfolding of this life within you, practise it on those who are nearest to you by meeting them with love and sympathy in the daily paths of life. Not only those whom you like, but those you care not for as well; not with those who love you only, but with those who dislike you also. Remember that you have to break down barriers—barriers of the bodies that bar you out from your fellow Selves in the worlds around you, and that breaking down of the barriers is part of the training in the spiritual life. Only as barrier after barrier is broken down, only as wall after wall is levelled to the ground, will the freedom of the Spirit become possible in manifestation on every plane and in every world. The Spirit is ever free in his own nature and his own life, but, confined within the barriers of the body, he has to learn to transcend them, before, on these planes of matter, he can realise the divine freedom which is his eternal birthright. So long as you feel yourself separate from others, so long are you shut out from the realisation of the unity; so long as you say "my" and "mine," so long the realisation of the Spirit is not yet possible for you. Love of individual possessions, not only physical but moral and mental, not the vulgar pride of physical wealth only, but moral pride, intellectual pride, everything that says "I" as against "you," and does not realise that I and you are one—all this is against the spiritual life. Hardest of all lessons when brought down to practical life; most difficult of all attainments when effort is made to realise it, and not only to talk about it and imagine it. It is best practised by continual renunciation of the individual possessions on every plane, and the constant thought of unity.

When you are trying to live the life of the Spirit, you will try to be pure. You do well, but why? In order that you may be pure, and leave your impure brethren in their impurity? Oh no! You must try to be pure, in order that there may be more purity in the world to share amongst all men, because you are pure. You are not wanting to be purer than others, but only gathering purity that you may spread it in every direction, and most joyous when your own purity lifts someone from the mire, who is trampled into it under the feet of the world. You want to be wise. You do well; for wisdom is a splendid possession. But why? In order that you may look down on the ignorant and say: "I am wiser than thou," as the pure man might say: "I am holier than thou"? Oh no! but in order that the wisdom that you gather may enlighten the ignorant, and become theirs and not only yours. Otherwise it is no spiritual thing; for spirituality does not know "myself" and "others"; it only knows the One Self, of whom all forms are manifestations.

We dare not call ourselves spiritual until we have reached that point which none of us as yet has reached, for to reach it means to become a Christ. When, looking at the lowest and basest and most ignorant and vilest, we can say: "That is myself, in such-and-such a garb," and say it feeling it, rejoicing in it—because if there are two of you, and one is pure and the other impure, and the two are one, then neither is perfect, but both are raised above the level of the lowest—that is the true atonement, the real work of the Christ; and the birth of Christ within you means the willingness to throw down all walls of separation, and the stature of Christ within you means that you have accomplished it.

For the most part we claim our unity above; we do not take pride in claiming our unity below; we are glad to say, "Yes, I also am Divine; I am a Christ in the making; I am one with Him." Harder to say: "I am one with the lowest of my brethren, sharing with them the same Divine life." Yet our Divinity is only realised as we recognise that same Divinity in others. You may remember that exquisite story of Olive Schreiner, breathing the very essence first of the unspiritual, and then of the spiritual life. In the first case a woman, pure and spotless, her garments shining with whiteness, and her feet shod as with snow, went up to the Gates of Heaven and trod the golden streets. And as she trod them in her shining robes the angels shuddered back, and said: "See, her garments are blood-spotted, and her sandals are stained with mire and blood." From the throne the Christ asked: "Daughter, how is it that your garments are blood-spotted and your sandals stained?" And she answered: "Lord, I was walking in miry ways, and I saw a woman there down in the mire, and I stepped upon her that I might keep my sandals clean." The Christ and the angels vanished, and the woman fell from heaven, and wandered again in the miry ways of earth. Once again she came to the .heavenly portal and trod the golden streets, and this time she was not alone. Another woman was with her, and the garments of both were blood-flecked, and the sandals of both were stained with the mire and blood of earth. But the angels seeing them pass by, cried out: "See how whitely their garments shine! And see how white are their feet!" And the Christ, when they came before the throne, said: "How come ye here in garments that are soiled ?" And the answer came: "I saw this my sister trampled upon, and I bent down to lift her up, and in the picking of her up my garments were soiled, but I have brought her with me to Thy presence." And the Christ smiled and lifted them up beside Him, and the angels sang for joy. For it is not the sin and the shame that are shared that soil the garments of the Spirit, and leave upon it the mire of earth.

If, then, you would lead the spiritual life, go downwards as well as upwards. Feel your unity with the sinner as well as with the saint. For the only thing that makes you divine is the Spirit that lives in every human heart alike, in all equally dwelling, and there is no difference in the divinity of the Spirit, but only in the stage of its manifestation. And just as you and I climb upwards and show more of the spiritual life in the lower worlds, should we raise our brethren with us, and know the joy of the redeemer, and the power of the life that saves. For Those whom we call Masters, Those who are the Christs of the world, Those are reverenced and beloved, because to Them there is no difference, but the sinner is as beloved as the saint—nay, sometimes more, because compassion flows out to the weaker more than to the strong.

Such is the spiritual life? such the goal that every man who would become spiritual must place before his eyes. Very different from the psychic, and not to be confused with it—the unfolding of the divinity in man, and not the purification and the organisation of the vehicles. Both are good, both necessary, and I finish with the words with which I began, that while to be psychic is no proof of spirituality, to be spiritual is to possess every power in heaven and on earth. Choose ye each your road. Tread whichever you will, but beware that by the growth of your powers here, in separation, you do not delay the growth of the spirituality which is the realisation of the unity of the Self. For everything which divides becomes evil, by the very fact of its dividing; every power which is shared is a wing to carry us upwards, but every power that is kept for the lower self is a clog that holds us down to earth.

www.ingramcontent.com/pod-product-compliance
Lightning Source LLC
LaVergne TN
LVHW041635070426
835507LV00008B/642